ONE
AND
ONLY

CLAIRE ELIZABETH GROSE

Copyright © 2022 by Claire Elizabeth Grose

Compiled and edited by Michael Grose and June Kennedy

All rights reserved. No portion of this publication may be reproduced, stored in a retrieval system or transmitted in any form by any means – electronic, mechanical, photocopying, recording, or any other –except for brief quotation in printed reviews, without the prior written permission of the publisher.

Unless indicated otherwise, all scripture quotations in this book are from the following source:

The Good News Bible: The Bible in Today's English Version (TEV) © 1976 by the American Bible Society. Used with permission.

ISBN 978-0-6486884-6-4

Author contact information - clairegrose.heartmatters@gmail.com

Version 1.0

DEDICATION

This book is dedicated to Carol and Dennis
My beloved sister and brother-in-law

CONTENTS

DEDICATION IV

CONTENTS V

PREFACE VIII

ACKNOWLEDGEMENTS X

    PART ONE 1

        MY DAILY PRAYER 4

        MY JESUS 5

        A LOVE THAT GROWS 6

        THE LORD'S BEAUTY 7

        BEING HERE WITH YOU 8

        SPRING IS RIPE 9

        WONDERS OF YOUR LOVE 10

        SUPER MOON 11

        BLOOM AND BLOSSOM 14

        SPRING PERFUME 15

        WHEN GOD MOVES THE SOUL 16

        PERFECT TUNE 17

        YOUR LOVE IS AROUND US 18

        PRECIOUS 19

        BREATHE LIFE 20

        A NEW YEAR STARTS 21

        TODAY 22

        BLESSINGS 23

        MY POURING PEN 26

        A REVELATION WITH GOD 27

        HEART SET EYES 28

        WAIT ON THE LORD 29

    PART TWO 30

        ONE AND ONLY 33

        BY YOUR SIDE 34

        HALLOWED TREASURE 35

        I'M WAITING IN YOUR LOVE 36

MY WORLD TODAY	37
FEED MY HEART	38
TEARDROP LOVE	41
YOUR HEAVENLY TOUCH	42
THE HAND OF FRIENDSHIP	43
HIS SOOTHING BALM	44
TAKE YOUR HEART TO HIS THRONE	45
I LOVE YOU IN ALL WAYS	46
THE FAMILY HE GAVE TO ME	49
HIS LOVE IS FOR ALL	50
EVERY DAY IS A LESSON	51
BE MY BEST	52
SHOW HIS LOVE	53
I'M IN YOUR PRECIOUS HANDS	54
IMPRESSION OF WORDS	57
SEE CLEARLY	58
ON YOU I CAN RELY	59
CALL ON THE RISEN LORD	60
KNOW HUMILITY	61
SHROUD ME	62
STEP INTO HIS LIGHT	63
THEE	64
ON CALL	65
HEAVENLY LOVE	66
SUSTAIN ME TODAY	67
DISTANT FEELING	68
PART THREE	69
ALPHA AND OMEGA	72
GOD'S PRESENCE	73
TESTING TIMES	74
PURE TRINITY	75
LET YOUR SPIRIT SHINE	76
SEEING THE LORD FOR THE FIRST TIME	77
VEIL OF GRACE	80
SPIRIT WORDS	81

- UNSPEAKABLE JOY 82
- SURRENDER TO JESUS 83
- HIS GIFTS ARE ENDLESS 84
- IGNITE YOUR FLAME 85

PART FOUR 86
- SACRIFICIAL CUP 89
- GOOD ENOUGH FOR A PARDON 90
- MY SOUL MATE 91
- THE LORD'S BELOVED 94
- LAMB OF GOD 95
- THE WONDER OF CHRISTMAS 98
- CHRISTMAS EVERY DAY 99
- A CHRISTMAS CANDLE 100
- MESSIAH OF HEAVEN AND EARTH 101

PREFACE

Two things I just wanted to say about this book are, why I started writing and how I came by the title.

I grew up in the 1950's-1960's in Adelaide, South Australia, my life was pretty simple but wonderful. I was very lucky to have a secure family life, and my Mum and Dad brought the family up to treat others with respect, do the right thing, be courteous, and respect your elders. We had a strict upbringing and even as adults our parents never criticized us but encouraged us to do our best in life. They were "Aussie battlers" but we always managed to make it through the tough times!

They were people of integrity and cared about others and instilled that into our family.

Church was a big part of our lives growing up. We went to Sunday School at an early age and progressed up through the appropriate groups as we got older.

Youth groups, camps and church anniversaries were all important to the whole family. We competed in church sports teams, basketball and tennis with other parishes across Adelaide. Life-long friendships were in the making and cherished golden memories to look back on that would never fade.

Bible stories, hymns and choruses were all part of getting to know Jesus. This nurturing finally led me to the day Jesus came knocking on my heart's door. Being filled with the Holy Spirit is something I will never forget and the overwhelming power of His love that filled my whole being and propelled me to the front of the hall to give my heart to Him. No words can fully describe the joy I felt. That was in February 1968, I was 14 years of age. He has been my Shining Light ever since, and lives within me always.

So I thank my beautiful Mum and Dad for the way they raised me and for the foundation of knowing Jesus' love.

It was in His love that I started to write, in the autumn of 1993. My journey has brought me to this book "One and Only", there is no one else like Him in all creation.

"Through him God made all things; not one thing in all creation was made without him." John 1:3 Good News Bible.

The title came to me when I was thinking of how to describe the Lord as I see Him. He is the one and only Son of God, who left His Throne of Glory to become a human just like us, through the miracle of His birth by Mary.

When I was a young Christian reading my Bible was really important to me in getting to know Jesus as my personal Saviour and became the foundation that I built my faith on.

It gave me strength and courage as I began life in the workforce at the age of 16. Coming from a sheltered upbringing it was my lifeline to self-confidence and adapting to social life at work.
The poems reflect the everyday feelings and emotions that we feel as we meet the challenges of life and how the great magnitude of God's love can help us rise above them.

I pray you will turn to Him not only in your hour of need but in celebration of happy times in your everyday life. He longs to be your Saviour and confidante so you can share everything with Him. The "One and Only" God Himself!

Many of these writings have been my first words of whispered prayer, so much that I have been moved to write them down at once and continue on in His wonderful and absolute love.

Together we write as He provides my inspiration.

All glory to Him, my precious Lord Jesus!

ONE AND ONLY

ACKNOWLEDGEMENTS

My heartfelt thanks to my beloved family, my Mum and Dad, Lilly and Ken, and my siblings Jeanette, June, Carol, Gloria and Lynne, for their never ending encouragement and support to me. To the rest of the family, you are all a precious link that joins us together.

To Michael and Andrew for your continual support to me in fulfilling my passion of writing poems for the Lord to help others through His Word.

A huge thank you to Junie for editing my poems and the coffees and lunches we enjoyed along the way.

To Joy Furnell for her Crown of Thorns drawing, you have an amazing gift, thank you Joy.

Special thanks to Carol for the glorious cover photo of Moraine Lake, Banff National Park, Alberta, Canada.

A big thank you to Michael, June and Hugh, Lynne and Eileen for photos also.

To my friends and Church Families, thank you for your love and support.

To my beautiful sons, Michael and Andrew, thank you for loving me, and I am so glad He gave you to me. I will love you forever. To your partners Andrea and Bianca and also my grandchildren, Ashleigh, Costa, Lailah and Jaxon, I love you all so much.

To you the reader, thank you for picking this book up and I pray you will find His peace and love on the pages ahead.

May He shower you all with His love and blessings.

PART ONE

"He reflects the brightness of God's glory and is the exact likeness of God's own being, sustaining the universe with his powerful word…"

Hebrews 1 : 3

ONE AND ONLY

THE ONE...
THE ONLY...

"...He is feeding his flock in the garden and gathering lilies."

Song of Songs 6 : 2

ONE AND ONLY

MY DAILY PRAYER

Be with me, stay with me,
Close by my side,
Fill me with your peace and love,
So my spirit shall surely fly
To the heights in your love,
As only you can give,
Prepare me for this day ahead,
So in me you'll always live.

MY JESUS

My Jesus is my Saviour,
Long ago He touched my life,
He opened my heart
To reveal His shining light.

My Jesus never leaves me,
He never tires of my requests,
His Spirit brings His love,
He's my Counsellor and Friend.

I see Him in the sunrise,
Rolling seas and setting sun,
High majestic mountains,
Springtime colour brings His love.

My Jesus is my Lord,
He rules over Heaven and Earth,
Lover of my soul,
One day He will return.

My Jesus is my Shepherd,
Hallowed He'll always be,
My Saviour, Lord and Master,
The risen Christ for me!

A LOVE THAT GROWS

I just grow deeper in Your love,
For You are love divine,
Contentment keeps on growing
Like the branches on a vine.

Your pure love I feel
When I'm centred with You,
My cares I can leave
Because I want to.

My heart is nurtured
By Your Spirit alone
Who brings You in great magnitude
To my spiritual home.

I grow deeper in Your love
When I seek Your calm and peace
In this paradise I found
Where You bring me to my knees.

THE LORD'S BEAUTY

The prettiest flower,
A golden sunset,
The whitest snowflake,
Soaring mountain tops,
The greenest valley,
A fresh sea breeze,
A stunning sunrise,
Autumn leaves.

His world around so beautiful,
We can stop and wonder,
It magnifies His glorious name,
His beauty we can ponder,
Glorify His wondrous name,
Stop and look around
At His awesome creation,
His beauty will be found.

BEING HERE WITH YOU

Wherever you are; He is,
A never ending presence
Within your life forever,
The King of Kings of Heaven.

Being here with You
In my daily life,
Surrendering all to You,
To me feels so right.

My precious King of Heaven,
Glorious in every way,
The Star of the Universe
Takes my breath away.

Being here with You
Is sanctuary at its best,
In our quiet times alone,
My heart You come to bless.

SPRING IS RIPE

The joy of beautiful spring,
The earth comes to life,
Sleeping through winter
Now spring is ripe.

Glorious buds break through
Bursting to show
Their heavenly colours,
The Saviour's gift, I know.

Endless Joy and splendour
Come to bless our hearts,
The soul soars in wonder,
His beauty plays a part.

Spring is ripe for the feast,
In glorious shapes and forms,
Time to reap her harvest,
His wealth on earth is born.

WONDERS OF YOUR LOVE

Thank You Lord for charging me
With Your love that sets me free,
And to be mindful of Your loving care
That brings Heaven's harmony.

A path to Your peaceful glades,
Fields of green and waterways,
Flowing gently in trickling streams,
Waterfalls are a wonder to me.

Chords and warbles fill the air,
Oh so sweet to take me where
Morning mist lifts to the heights,
From warmth of day to frosty nights.

Soothing sounds are all around
When I stop to hear,
Your wonders that You made for me
To bring me love and cheer.

Quiet sea lies flat and calm
Reflecting clouds above,
Mirror finish proudly shows
The wonders of Your love.

SUPER MOON

Your glory and Your wonder
As Super Moon comes close to earth,
In the night sky above
We can see her heavenly worth.

Shining bright and glorious,
The biggest she can get,
She changes her position,
The best we've seen her yet.

Super Moon so bright,
On a clear night we see
Her beauty and her wonder,
She was made by Thee.

So thank You Lord for Super Moon
And the wonder of her light,
When she comes close to earth
On a starry night!

ONE AND ONLY

ONE AND ONLY

WONDERS OF HIS HAND…

"the Creator of heaven, earth, and sea,
and all that is in them…"

Psalm 146 : 6

BLOOM AND BLOSSOM

Bloom and blossom in His love
That is sweet through and through,
It comes with His anointing
To truly bless you.

Bloom and blossom in His love
A love so divine,
Coming from the Father,
The one precious vine.

Bloom and blossom in His love,
Like a flower's perfect form,
Pure love in all its fullness,
In Him you are reborn.

Bloom and blossom in His Spirit,
His gift that is yours,
So precious and overwhelming
Like the awakening of the dawn.

SPRING PERFUME

Morning song so sweet,
The Master hears them all,
Peace reigns supreme,
Every morning's wake-up call.

Birds nourish the flowers
Without a human hand
To generate growth
And be harvested by man.

Perfume sweet remains
To fill our senses so,
Spring in all her fullness,
The best she can show.

Spring brings new life to everything,
What joy it surely is,
Around the world this season,
Mother Nature so complete.

WHEN GOD MOVES THE SOUL

When the soul is moved by God,
Great things happen to the heart,
His Holy Spirit moves,
You will make a new start.

You will know divine love
In fullness so complete,
Your cup will overflow
At His mercy seat.

When God moves your soul
A new life begins,
You can't believe the change
That's happening within.

Your conscience will step forth
In faith and truth,
Your heart will reveal
A love that is brand new.

When God moves the soul,
Heaven comes to stay,
Jesus lives within,
You are on your way.

PERFECT TUNE

Stars beyond our reach
Hang in space above,
Placed with sun and moon,
Made with eternal love.

Touchable only
By God's holy hand,
You placed them above
To fulfil Your holy plan.

Thank You Lord
For this precious earth,
Where wonders abound
For us to observe.

You made the earth
In perfect tune,
Your creation in time,
That once was brand new.

YOUR LOVE IS AROUND US

We see Your love around us
In Your creation everywhere,
It's in the plants and flowers
For us all to share.

We see Your love around us
In a friendly face or smile,
Such a simple thing
Can make our day worthwhile.

So thank You Lord
For the friends who care
And the love they bring
We can take anywhere.

PRECIOUS

Precious Holy Father
Always be mine,
You speak to the heart,
Your Words I have to find.

Precious Holy Saviour,
You want each soul to know
How much You love them,
Your Word tells us so.

You taught us how to live
And showed us how to pray,
Dearest Holy Lord
Be with me today.

Almighty King of Kings,
We are precious in Your sight,
You will always be
The Way, the Truth and the Life.

BREATHE LIFE

The human heart beats with life,
Life You breathed within,
To each soul on the earth
Where their story begins.

You made us in Your image
And gave us Your breath,
Our life was already written
Before it even began.

You know our every move
And You gave us freedom of choice,
Help us to choose what's right
And to listen to Your voice.

Yes, You gave us the breath of life Lord,
In our mother's womb we were formed,
Be with us all our days Lord,
Watch over us 'til the dawn.

A NEW YEAR STARTS

Wipe the slate clean
Inside your heart,
Start from today
As the New Year starts.

Move on to a clean slate,
Have new hope in your heart,
All things are possible,
With God is where you can start.

Yes, as the New Year begins,
Carry trust and faith as you journey,
What will the future bring?
Walk in God's grace and mercy.

TODAY

And so the circle continues
By His holy hand,
We only have today
To work through His plan.

Everything has a reason
At first we may not see,
When passing through today
We will see reality.

With the Saviour in our hearts
He will brighten every day,
The owner of our soul,
We only have today.

BLESSINGS

Thank You for Your blessings Lord
That continue to flow
Into my heart
Because I love You so.

I pray for Your peace and calm
To abide with me each day,
I need Your shield to protect me
As I journey on my way.

Sometimes I feel lost,
That's when I spill my heart over You,
Your Spirit comes close
To make me feel brand new.

My patch on earth complete
Because You are here,
Your Spirit brings Your blessings,
He brings You oh so near.

ONE AND ONLY

FIND DELIGHT IN THE LORD…

"Who is this whose glance is like the dawn?..."

Song of Songs 6 : 10

MY POURING PEN

My pouring pen flows with His love,
A love that knows no end,
For all people of the world,
A love His Spirit sends.

My pouring pen flows anytime
And also anywhere,
Day or night it's with me,
His wondrous love I share.

I write His Words to the world
So they will receive His gift
To accept Him into their heart,
So forever they will live.

My pouring pen runs like a river
Sometimes fast, sometimes slow,
Be sure these words will come
From the Saviour who loves us so.

My pouring pen is for His lambs
And those who want to come,
His kingdom is forever more
To receive God's only Son.

A REVELATION WITH GOD

A revelation with God
Known only to you,
Will turn your life around,
This is so true.

A mountain top experience
That you just can't stop,
Your thoughts submerged
In heaven's glorious loft.

The Lord Himself
Who will come into your heart,
Will baptize you with His Spirit,
That's where your revelation starts.

A revelation with God
Doesn't come by every day,
Take His hand and surrender
To His love that never fades.

HEART SET EYES

When my heart is set
On something I desire,
Lord give me Your grace
To set my sight higher.

Your will for me
No man can ever change,
Keep my heart set eyes
On Heaven's lofty range.

I can only wait
Until the days end
To see if my heart's desire
Has been Heaven sent.

So, precious Saviour keep
My heart set eyes on You,
To wait for Your prompts
So I see Your point of view.

WAIT ON THE LORD

The future lies before you,
Uncertainty reigns,
You can only take one day at a time
As you go on your way.

If you wait on the Lord
With trust in your heart,
Make Him your foundation
That's where you can start.

His mercy and grace
Will shower you every day,
Be open to His gifts
That come your way.

Wait on the Lord,
Strength and courage He'll supply,
Tell Him your every need,
On Him you can rely.

Continue on your journey,
Wait on the Lord,
In Him you'll have everything,
He's the one you'll adore.

PART TWO

"…a voice said from heaven,
"This is my own dear Son, with whom I am pleased."

Matthew 3 : 17

ONE AND ONLY

HE LEFT HIS HEAVENLY REALM…
SO WE COULD BE HIS FAMILY…

"The Word became a human being and, full of grace and truth, lived among us…"

John 1 : 14

ONE AND ONLY

The one and only is my Lord
Who loves so ceaselessly,
Each one of us on this earth,
He came that we'd be free.

Free from sin completely,
When we confess we believe in Him,
He paid the price at Calvary
So through Him we can live.

One and only Kingship,
In His hands we are held,
Centre of creation,
The Saviour of the world.

One and only Son divine,
Your authority reigns,
You control the universe,
Holy is Your Name!

BY YOUR SIDE

He will change you into His likeness,
You will care for your fellow man,
His love will consume you
Then you will understand.

He will never leave you,
By your side He'll always stay,
He longs for your heart
To open to be saved.

You'll have a friend forever,
Through the ups and downs of life,
He'll be there to help you
Through the days and nights.

You'll never be lonely,
The King of Kings is by your side,
The crown He carries in His hands,
Will be yours in ageless time.

HALLOWED TREASURE

Hallowed treasure is the Lord Himself
And His love divine,
He will dwell within your soul,
He will make your heart shine.

Hallowed treasure is yours to take
When you seek Him as your own,
Claim Him as your Saviour,
You will never be alone.

In His likeness you will be changed,
Your thoughts and heart will know,
Compassion and kindness will own you,
His love you will show.

You will have eternal life
When you claim His hallowed treasure,
Your old ways will disappear
He will change you forever.

I'M WAITING IN YOUR LOVE

Help me to be patient Lord
For Your will to come to pass,
Though many days will rise
Until I know my path.

The greatest blessing of all
Is that Your will be done,
Here on earth
As it is above.

I'm waiting in Your love,
I feel Your hand divine
Gently guiding me,
I'll love You for all time.

Give me strength to cope
With my future ahead,
Precious Lord be with me,
Help me strive to do my best.

MY WORLD TODAY

The dawn awakes
My world for today,
All I know Lord
Is I need You this day.

I try not to look
Too far ahead,
I'm just living today,
Step by step.

I can't carry the hours ahead,
The load is too heavy to bear,
The contents of my heart Lord
With You I have to share.

Give me strength to get through today,
The hours are long and slow,
All I know is, I love You Lord,
I want You to know.

I surrender my life to You,
Forgive me for my ways,
All I know is Lord,
I need You this day.

FEED MY HEART

Feed my heart with Your love
To sustain the hunger in me,
Your mercy and grace
Truly sets me free.

Feed my heart with Your love,
A love that never ends,
A flame burning bright
That Your Holy Spirit sends.

Feed my heart with Your love,
So goodwill I can sow,
For Your message to reach
The ones that need it so.

Feed my heart to the brim
With Your pure love,
So Your joy will be mine
Through Your Holy Spirit's touch.

ONE AND ONLY

NO MOUNTAIN TOO HIGH…
NO CARE TOO DEEP…

"…He comes running over the mountains, racing across the hills to me."

Song of Songs 2 : 8

TEARDROP LOVE

The Lord sends teardrop love,
To fall so tenderly,
Shining like a diamond
To hearts that have heard His plea.

Arriving to bless,
Descending deep to the soul,
Pure teardrop love
Makes your spirit whole.

Precious teardrop love
Washes pain away,
Leaving shining pearls
That will never fade.

Teardrop love form Heaven,
A never ending flow
Into the heart forever,
To make you white as snow.

YOUR HEAVENLY TOUCH

Your heavenly touch so potent Lord,
Our understanding can never know
That the power of Your hand
Still heals the deepest blow.

There's nothing like Your touch
When we surrender to You,
Your goodness will prevail,
No matter what we do.

You can give hope to the desperate,
You can soften the toughest heart,
You turn a frown to a smile
And You can meet a need worthwhile.

In You we have forgiveness,
A never ending love,
When we submit to Your touch
Into the heart You'll surely come.

Yes, Your heavenly touch is power
Straight from Your Throne
Where You reside in Glory
Our forever home.

THE HAND OF FRIENDSHIP

Hold out the hand of friendship
When you're in God's house,
That's where it begins,
It will continue no doubt.

The hand of friendship
Will prompt you to serve,
The act of caring
Speaks louder than words.

The world itself
Has scars so deep,
We need the hand of friendship
To help those in need.

The hand of friendship,
Christ longs to see
His beloved caring
For all His family.

HIS SOOTHING BALM

His soothing balm will heal and mend
Your deepest wound within,
For peace and calm to reside,
His presence He will bring.

His soothing balm will anoint your heart
So His glory will remain
To always comfort you
Each time will be your gain.

His soothing balm brought by His Spirit
So special and divine,
He brings Heaven's blessings
To help you just in time.

His soothing balm so sweet and pure
Waits for your request,
Ask the Saviour to heal you,
In Him you will find rest.

TAKE YOUR HEART TO HIS THRONE

Your story isn't easy,
Words fail to rise
From lips that are quiet,
You just want to hide.

Emotion is deep,
That rules the day,
But you can overcome it
When you lift your gaze.

Lift your eyes to the Saviour,
Take your heart to His Throne
Where His love abides,
He will take your load.

Though your focus is deep,
Your thoughts tell you so,
Lift your eyes to the Saviour,
Take your heart to His Throne.

Claim His help today
You are not alone,
He will come to you,
Take your heart to His Throne.

I LOVE YOU IN ALL WAYS

I love You in all ways
In my heart, mind and soul,
But my heart must be open
To receive Your lessons told.

I love You in all ways,
Even when I feel no charge,
My faith is still the same,
I trust Your open arms.

I love You in all ways,
Though my body grows weak,
Life can be difficult
The Spirit's help I seek.

I love You in all ways
To direct my path in life,
Your Spirit will prompt me
With Your shining light.

KING OF KINGS...
LORD OF LORDS...

"...His name is greater than all others;
His glory is above earth and heaven."

Psalm 148 : 13

THE FAMILY HE GAVE TO ME

Sometimes life seems empty
As we look back over the years,
In our prime life was hectic,
Where did they go those years?

Memories flood back from yesterday
As clear as can be,
My childhood and teenage years
Were so wonderful for me.

A simple but wonderful life
We had growing up,
Battlers through the years
But we always had enough.

Love and respect were utmost
As we shared each other's hurts,
Which we made "a matter of prayer"
Left in God's hands where they were nursed!

So I look back with much love
On the family He gave to me,
I couldn't have been happier,
Precious links we always will be.

HIS LOVE IS FOR ALL

His love is for all
People of the world,
Every nation He created
It evolved at His call.

No matter where you live
Across the world so wide,
You can receive His gift
To live in ageless time.

His love is for all,
Only the heart can feel
What your spiritual eyes see,
Is love that makes you kneel.

His love is for all,
Divine and so complete,
To those who believe
In His Holy Trinity.

EVERY DAY IS A LESSON

Every day is a lesson,
Sometimes it's what we know,
Other days we can learn,
Our journey tells us so.

Every day is a lesson,
We know not what will come,
Some days nothing changes
But we all have different ones.

We hope for happy days,
To stay in our comfort zone
But sometimes we stray
Outside and feel alone.

The Saviour is always with us,
So we have to claim His help,
Every day is a lesson,
To His strength you can help yourself.

BE MY BEST

I just have to keep coming back
For You to refill my cup,
I need You to sustain me Lord
For all my days to come.

I think I am strong
But when it comes to the test,
Situations give me cause
To not always feel my best.

Doubts and fears rise up
To consume my every thought,
They interrupt my peace
That Your Spirit brought.

So I ask dear Lord for Your strength
Every day of my life,
So I can be my best,
Because I'm precious in Your sight.

SHOW HIS LOVE

Christ came to give us
The greatest gift of all,
A divine precious Life,
One for many was the call.

In Him we have forgiveness,
No more scorn or misery,
For He is the Light,
He will bring harmony.

His love will overwhelm you,
Your heart washed pure and clean
When you accept the Saviour,
You will know sincerity.

He will live within you,
His love you will own,
When you know the Saviour
His love you will show.

I'M IN YOUR PRECIOUS HANDS

I'm in Your precious hands Lord,
Loving me with pure love,
Your hands that made the world
And placed the stars above.

I'm in Your precious hands,
Pierced from the nails at Calvary,
You took my place that day,
A sinner that was me.

I'm in Your precious hands,
They wipe my tears away,
When my whispers call
"Lord come to me this day".

I'm in Your precious hands
When my body grows weak,
You'll carry me precious Lord,
In my time of need.

ONE AND ONLY

DAWN AND SUNSET…
ARE THE JEWELS IN HIS CROWN…

"…But on you the light of the Lord will shine;
The brightness of his presence will be with you."

Isaiah 60 : 2

IMPRESSION OF WORDS

Forgive us Lord for our selfishness
When feelings get out of control,
In time may we remember
To forgive and not to scold.

Our fragile hearts feel the knocks
From words that are said,
Maturity will mellow
Our thoughts before they're said.

As we grow older
We can change our thoughts in time,
Words can leave a great impression,
Always the choice is mine.

So keep counsel with the Holy One
To help us choose our words,
May they be heartfelt and worthy
To always be heard.

SEE CLEARLY

Some days I don't see clearly Lord,
My world overrides thoughts of You,
But when I try and focus
I feel comforted by You.

I can rise above my doubts
That come to control,
With thoughts of You in mind
You lift my heart and soul.

To look above the fog
That can hang around for days,
I only have to ask You
To take it all away.

I can see You more clearly,
You revive me in Your love,
My thoughts restored again
Because when I call You come.

ON YOU I CAN RELY

On You I can rely Lord
In every way,
Give me the strength
In Your love, mercy and grace.

On You I can rely,
I am in Your hands,
My trust secure,
For You have made my plans.

You never leave me Lord,
I have You by my side,
You are always there,
On You I can rely.

Being in Your service Lord,
A privilege indeed,
On You I can rely Lord,
I will sow eternal seeds.

CALL ON THE RISEN LORD

Call on the risen Lord,
Step outside your comfort zone,
Look to your soul
That He truly owns.

Reach for His Word
For stamina and pace,
All the answers to life
You will find on every page.

His grace is so complete
To all who call on Him,
He's waiting for your whispers
To invite Him within.

Call on the risen Lord
To heal you with His balm,
His sweetness you will know
In His open arms.

KNOW HUMILITY

Take a step back
And look ahead,
Think before you act
So a tear won't be shed.

We may be tough on the outside
From the world's point of view,
But inside our heart can crumble
In a second or two.

In the Saviour's eyes we are equal,
To Him we are all worthy,
He took the Cross for our pardon
So we could receive His grace and mercy.

The Saviour is our Holy Teacher,
Only He is without sin,
Look to the Master today
For humility within.

SHROUD ME

Lord, shroud me in Your grace,
Take my fears and doubts
Make me worthy to see Your face,
Those I can live without.

Shroud me in Your peace,
For hearts to receive,
So they will know eternal calm
When they step into Your open arms.

Shroud me in Your joy
Then I can take from Your store,
Loving You I will receive
Your Eternal life and more.

Loving Lord shroud me
So Your face I will see,
Hold me close forever more,
It's You I'm waiting for.

STEP INTO HIS LIGHT

Stay strong in His light,
Come close to His Throne,
Walk in His shadow,
You will never be alone.

Strength will find you
For the road ahead,
Courage will step forward,
You will be led.

In His light
You will find your steps,
Leaving fears behind,
His guidance He will send.

So step into His light
Where you can never fail,
His rays will reach for you,
His light will never pale.

ONE AND ONLY

THEE

You are the precious Holy Father
Who created all we see,
Owner of the universe,
You bring us to our knees.

You made each beating heart,
You know the life within,
No fingerprint is the same
In the world we live.

Your power is unimaginable,
No mortal can conceive
Until we pass to Glory
And present to Thee.

Your divine Holy Spirit
You gave us to reveal
Your love in all its fullness,
Our great Comforter and Shield!

ON CALL

My counsellor, my Lord
Is always on call
To help with the slightest need,
When I trip or fall.

I don't know when my emotions
Will run high or low,
I need my dear Saviour
To surely steady the flow.

I only have to ask
And claim my need,
He responds at the time
For my heart to follow His lead.

He answers every prayer,
Not always to my plan,
But my Saviour is always on call,
To lead me by the hand.

HEAVENLY LOVE

To know Christ's heavenly love
No greater gift can be,
In Him we are consumed by holiness,
Each spirit will be free.

His gift to every heart
Who confesses Him Lord,
And believes He died on the Cross
The sins for many He bore.

He is the one and only
Who is perfect love,
He shines brighter than the sun
In heaven above.

His love is our foundation
For eternal life,
In Him we are forgiven
We are precious in His sight.

His love is pure joy,
Only the soul truly knows,
Accept the risen Christ,
So His Spirit to you can flow.

SUSTAIN ME TODAY

I live in Your love,
I walk in Your light,
Precious Holy Father
Hold me tight.

I need Your love
To sustain me today,
I can't make it alone,
I need You today.

Life brings its doubts,
What will tomorrow bring?
I will do the best I can,
I trust You, my King.

Keep me strong in Your love,
Take my fears and my doubts,
Sustain me dear Lord,
You; I can't live without.

DISTANT FEELING

Sometimes You seem distant Lord
But I still look for Thee,
No matter how I feel,
It's You I want to see.

I don't like that distant feeling,
I like You up close,
To feel Your presence around me
Is what I love the most.

So take that distant feeling Lord,
I know my world is to blame,
Help me to rise above it,
I still worship You the same.

I know my worries get in the way
But please Lord have Your say
Take that distant feeling Lord
I need You every day.

PART THREE

"I am the first and the last," says the Lord God Almighty, who is, who was, and who is to come."

Revelation 1 : 8

ONE AND ONLY

ALL POWER AND GLORY...
ARE HIS...

"Christ is the visible likeness of the invisible God.
He is the first- born Son, superior to all created things.
For through him God created everything in heaven and on earth,
the seen and the unseen things, including spiritual powers,
lords, rulers, and authorities. God created the whole
universe through him and for him."

Colossians 1 : 15 - 16

ALPHA AND OMEGA

The Alpha and the Omega,
You own the universe,
Your light shines of salvation
Because You were the first.

The Alpha and the Omega,
Precious Lord You are,
You made eternity
And the morning and evening star.

The Alpha and the Omega,
You are the Holy One,
Divine almighty King of Kings,
Sacred Holy Son.

The Alpha and the Omega,
We exist at Your behest,
Owner of creation,
The beginning and the end.

GOD'S PRESENCE

Come into God's presence
Reverently in prayer,
You can meet Him daily
To share your heartfelt cares.

There's nothing you can't tell Him,
Your cares He longs to hold,
Whether they are big or small
Each one He will resolve.

Come into God's presence
With respect and openly
Confess your heart's desire,
He loves you endlessly.

Find your peace and calm
From the clamour of the world,
Come into God's presence,
Be happy in yourself.

He wants to bring you joy
Every day of your life,
Come into God's presence,
Be filled with His light.

TESTING TIMES

Challenges come along in life
To test our faith and trust,
Will you take it to the Lord?
For His will to come to pass.

Can you keep your peace and calm
Amidst the testing times?
Take it to the Lord in prayer,
His help you will find.

Testing times will take you
Through the valleys in your life,
But through His Holy Spirit,
The way He will provide.

The question in testing times
Is "what do I do?"
Pray for His mercy and grace,
The answer will come to you.

It's in the testing times we grow,
Wounds and hurts can be healed,
Take everything to the Saviour
So His ways can be revealed.

PURE TRINITY

So sacred and so pure
God's Trinity: the Holy Hosts,
All power and glory,
The Father, Son and Holy Ghost.

How precious and divine,
Pure Trinity remains,
Throughout eternity,
Never changes, stays the same.

Their love will last forever,
Brought to earth by the Son,
The Father sent His Dearest
Because He is the only One.

The pure Trinity,
We can proclaim our Heavenly Hosts,
Blessed they remain,
Father, Son and Holy Ghost.

LET YOUR SPIRIT SHINE

Let Your Spirit shine Lord,
Forever a light,
Deep into my soul
Where I'm precious in Your sight.

Let Your Spirit shine
Out to the world,
A beacon for mankind
Who will accept Your Word?

Let Your Spirit shine
So they can have Eternity
In Your paradise above
That will bring tranquility.

Let Your Spirit shine
On my open heart,
A golden light forever
To keep me on Your path.

SEEING THE LORD FOR THE FIRST TIME

Seeing the Lord for the first time,
Wonder struck my soul,
Such rapture I've ever known,
His Glory I took hold.

Seeing the Lord for the first time,
His grace and mercy I received,
Commanding my all
Now He has set me free.

I can never be the same
Now the Saviour lives within,
Though life still has its shadows,
I keep my focus on Him.

Seeing Him for the first time,
His Holy Spirit shrouds my all,
Bringing His love in great magnitude,
I'm so glad I answered His call.

ONE AND ONLY

ALWAYS BY YOUR SIDE…

"God will put his angels in charge of you to protect you wherever you go."

Psalm 91 : 11

VEIL OF GRACE

Your wondrous gift of grace
Can make a soul brand new,
Pardoned we can approach Your Throne
When we give our heart to You.

We can surrender every care
Into Your pierced hands,
Your veil of grace will shroud
Each one that's in Your plan.

Each special soul upon this earth
Can wear Your veil of grace
That comes from love divine,
From Heaven's Holy place.

This special gift will equip us
Every day of our life,
A quality beyond words,
From Jesus, our shining light.

SPIRIT WORDS

Lord, help me to wait before You
To hear Your Spirit Words,
That will fall into my heart
Silently unheard.

My soul will react
With warmth from love so deep
That will change me forever
At Your Mercy Seat.

Your Spirit Words will come
From Your heart that can love the world,
That forgives each broken promise
And picks up each one who fell.

You'll forgive the deepest blow
That mankind can deal,
Because of Calvary
Eternal Life revealed.

Your Spirit Words forever sound
Through the centuries of time,
Are heard by Your beloved
To share with all mankind.

UNSPEAKABLE JOY

Unspeakable joy will come to you
When you take His Holy hand,
Words will be beyond you,
You will not understand.

Unspeakable joy will flow
And absorb your very soul,
When you know the Saviour
His glory will unfold.

You will know pure love
In its Holy state,
Only from the Master
Divine love you can take.

Unspeakable joy is yours
Your whole life through,
Take Him for your Saviour,
Unspeakable joy is waiting for you.

SURRENDER TO JESUS

Surrender to Jesus
All that is in your heart,
His tender hands will lead you,
On your daily path.

Ask Him for freedom
To place your cares in His hands,
He hears your pleas and whispers,
Only He understands.

He planned your life
A long time ago,
Release your concerns
To the one who truly knows.

Surrender to Jesus
For peace and calm within,
Your joy will overflow,
Give your cares to Him.

HIS GIFTS ARE ENDLESS

His gifts are endless
When we open our heart to Him,
Freely He will give
When we turn to Him.

His gifts are endless
When we rise above our fears,
Claim His help to overcome
He will surely come near.

His gifts are endless
When we surrender all to Him,
He longs for our attention,
So give your all to Him.

His gifts are endless,
They come from Eternity,
That's our home He has prepared
So with Him we'll always be.

IGNITE YOUR FLAME

Lord, ignite Your flame in my heart
To keep our love alive,
Freely You give to me
From Your Throne on high.

Ignite Your flame in my soul
Where Your Spirit shines
Ever so brightly
To thrill this heart of mine.

Ignite Your flame in my life
To keep me on track
And brighten my journey
So there's nothing I will lack.

Thank You Lord for Your flame
That burns brightly for the world,
In time may every heart
Accept Your eternal Word.

PART FOUR

"So he said to them, "When you lift up the
Son of Man, you will know that "I Am Who I Am";…

John 8 : 28

ONE AND ONLY

CALVARY...
TOOK OUR SIN...

"...John saw Jesus coming to him, and said,
"There is the Lamb of God, who takes away the sin of the world!"

John 1 : 29

SACRIFICIAL CUP

The sacrificial cup
Poured out for all mankind
By the Son of Man
Who gave His life for mine.

God gave His One and Only
Who obeyed His Father's will,
The Tree of Calvary
Today is still so real.

The sacrificial cup,
Holy precious Son,
Carried His Cross to a hill
Where He was lifted up.

He paid the price just once
For mankind to be free,
He lives, He lives today
Because of Calvary.

God raised His precious Son
On the third day from the Tomb,
Now He lives forever
In your heart, please give Him room.

GOOD ENOUGH FOR A PARDON

Are we good enough for a pardon Lord?
Our shame brings its doubts,
But You are love itself Lord,
That's what Calvary was about.

Are we good enough for a pardon Lord?
Our guilt surely says "no",
But on a hill at Calvary
A young Nazarene thought so!

He took our sin to Calvary,
It was His Father's call,
He was nailed to a wooden Cross,
He took the sin of all.

Yes, the Son of God came to earth
For that one day at Calvary
So we could have eternal life
And a pardon to receive!

For a pardon for every sin
We only have to believe
That He took the Cross for us,
And from death He rose to Victory!

MY SOUL MATE

My true soul mate; the Lord Jesus Christ,
Messiah of the world
Brought His peace and glory
The day He was upheld.

On a wooden Cross
That He carried Himself,
He was in agony
But it was our pain He felt.

Our sin took Him to Calvary
Because He loved us so,
He gave us Eternity
So His love we would know.

He wants to live in our hearts
So His peace we can pass along,
He is my soul mate today,
Let Him be yours; for you He longs.

ONE AND ONLY

AFTER HIS RESURRECTION…
JESUS APPEARS TO HIS DISCIPLES…

"As the sun was rising, Jesus stood at the water's edge, but the disciples did not know that it was Jesus."
"When they stepped ashore, they saw a charcoal fire there with fish on it and some bread."
"Jesus said to them, "Come and eat."…

John 21 : 4, 9, 12

THE LORD'S BELOVED

The whole world is Your beloved,
You crave for our lips to confess,
"You the King of Kings,
Come to me so I can live".

You love the whole world,
That You gave Your life for us,
On a Cross at Calvary
You were lifted up.

We are Your beloved,
Holy is Your Name,
You bear the marks of Calvary,
We can never be the same.

You forgave our sin that day,
To give us a place in Eternity,
Now You are seated by Your Father,
Your beloved we will always be.

LAMB OF GOD

I bow before Your Throne of Gold
Where You sit for all to behold,
By the Father You reside in time
In Your Word it is told.

Lamb of God Your Throne of Gold,
Heaven's most high above,
So sacred and divine,
I worship You in Holy love.

Lamb of God Your Throne of Gold,
In Your power and glory You reign,
Your angels bow down to worship You,
"Blessed" You remain.

My prayer for the world is to acknowledge You
The "Lamb of God " on Your Throne,
So they will have Eternal Life,
And make Your Throne their home.

WHAT JOY…
THE MIRACLE OF HIS BIRTH…

"…For it is by the Holy Spirit that she has conceived.
She will have a son, and you will name him Jesus…"

Matthew 1 : 20, 21

THE WONDER OF CHRISTMAS

The wonder of Christmas
The world celebrates
The birth of Christ Jesus
The Bethlehem Babe.

The wonder of Christmas
The angels brought forth,
Who sang with great gladness
"The birth of the Lord".

Humbly in a stable that wondrous night,
Worshipped by shepherds and the Magi,
Animals came too to worship the Lord,
The wonder of Christmas to adore.

Two thousand years on,
His birth still acclaimed,
The Messiah has come,
Let's worship His name.

CHRISTMAS EVERY DAY

The Lord born in a humble stable
Shrouded by a shining star,
Your power and Your glory
Your gift to every heart.

If Christmas could be every day
What a wonderful world it would be,
The joy that comes from giving,
Comes from eternity.

If Christmas could be every day
Goodwill would always be,
Reaching out to one another,
Happiness we would see.

To unite as one people,
How glorious life would be,
To worship the one Messiah,
Like the Magi on bended knee.

A CHRISTMAS CANDLE

Light a Christmas candle
For the Light of the World,
The Lord in all His glory
His story we have to tell.

His angels came to proclaim
His arrival that night,
The star shone high above
The Blessed Holy site.

Light a Christmas candle
To show His pure light,
His glory will shine forever
For you and I.

Light a Christmas candle
For the awe of the Lord,
The arrival of the Messiah
He couldn't love us more!

MESSIAH OF HEAVEN AND EARTH

Maker of all creation,
Everything in global space,
He made us in His image
So we can look upon His face.

Messiah of heaven and earth,
Saviour to the world,
His hands still heal from days of old
As His Bible stories tell.

Glorious divine Father,
Almighty to forgive,
Loves us unconditionally,
His Spirit He truly gives.

Messiah of heaven and earth
In Your glory angels bow,
We will know Your wonder
When the final Trumpet sounds.

Messiah of heaven and earth,
Holy is Your Name,
Every knee will bow
When we meet that glorious day!

ALSO BY CLAIRE GROSE

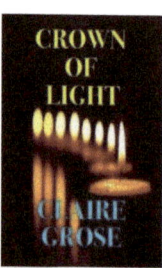

ABOUT THE AUTHOR

Claire worked as a Government Public Servant in the Lands Department, Adelaide, South Australia until she married and became a mother of two boys.

She later returned to the work force during which time she gained a "Living Hope" Phone Counselling certificate which influenced her need to help others.

Through this and personal experience she found herself inspired by God's love to put pen to paper.

PHOTO CREDITS

COVER PHOTO: Moraine Lake, Banff National Park, Alberta, Canada - taken by Carol Turner

Page 2: Magnolias; Maleny, Queensland – Claire Grose
Page 12: Penguins; Auckland Aquarium, New Zealand – Michael
Page 24: Bluff Beach; Yorke Peninsula, S.A. – Claire Grose
Page 31: Creek grasses; Lyndoch, S.A. – Lynne & Eileen
Page 39: Bougainvillea; Maleny, Queensland – Claire Grose
Page 47: Wallaman Falls; Queensland. – June and Hugh
Page 55: Rhine River; Germany. – Michael and Andrea
Page 70: River reeds; Mannum, S.A. – Claire Grose
Page 78: Windmill; Yorke Peninsula. S.A. – Claire Grose
Page 87: Pottery drawings for Claire Grose
Page 92: Eyre Peninsula S.A. – Claire Grose
Page 96: Watsonias; Mallala, S.A. – Lynne and Eileen

ONE AND ONLY